Easy Concertos and Concertinos
for Violin and Piano

O. Rieding

Concerto
in E minor

Op. 7
(1st to 7th position)

Bosworth

Concerto.

Oskar Rieding, Op.7.

B. & Cº 16653

6

Molto moderato.

Cadensa ad lib.

Allegro moderato.

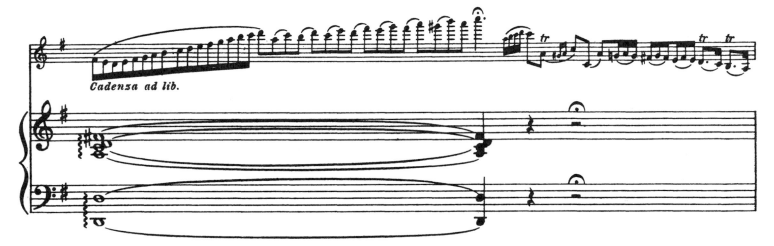

ritard.

a tempo

ritard.

a tempo

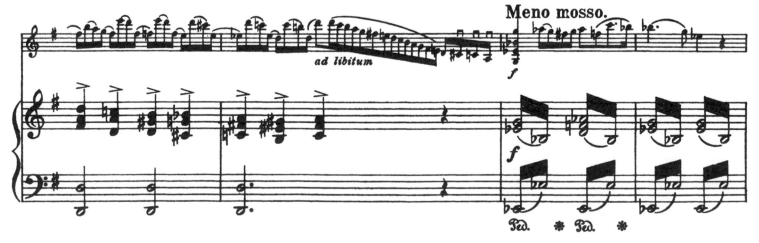

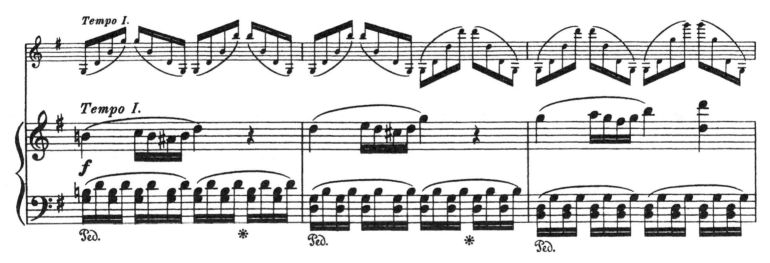

Concerto.

VIOLINO.

Oskar Rieding, Op. 7.

B. & C⁰ 16853

VIOLINO.

VIOLINO.

Molto moderato.

PUCK

MICHAEL KREIN

GIPSY CARNIVAL

VIOLIN

YASCHA KREIN

IMPROMPTU IN F

VIOLIN

JOSEPH DETHERIDGE (1848)

Ragamuffin

Fiddle-Polka

Spitzbub
Geigen-Polka

Fripon
Polka des violons

Violin

Quick Polka

Joe Rixner
Arr. L. J. Boer

Eight "Bagatellen."

VIOLIN.

Nº 4. Rondino.

Gustav Ellerton, Op. 16 Nº 4.

Allegro vivo.

GAVOTTE.

Violin.

Gustav Ellerton, Op. 21 Nº 3.

Leggiero e scherzando.

Souvenir de Capri.

Serenata.

Spieldauer | Durée | Duration } ca. 4 Min.

Violino Solo.

Giuseppe Becce, Op. 12ª
Componista della Serenata amorosa,
Legende d'Amour

Andante tranquillo. (sordina!)

Mazurka de Concert.

Introduction.
Moderato.

VIOLIN.

OVIDE MUSIN.

L. Portnoff

Russian Fantasia No. 1

Russian Fantasia No. 2

Russian Fantasia No. 3

Waving Fields

Slavonic Cradle-song

Minuet in old Style

Molto moderato.

Canzonetta.

Violin.

Christian Schäfer.

Lisette-!-
Mouvement de Valse.

Violino.

Guido Papini, Op. 47, No 3.

Sarabande.
A. Corelli.

VIOLINE.

Basil Althaus.

Giga.
A. Corelli.

Air Varié.

VIOLINO.

O. Rieding, Op. 23, No 2.

Danse des Libellules.
Libellentanz.
Dance of the Dragon Flies.

Violino.

Oscar Rieding, Op. 20.

Midnight Bells.
VIENNESE MELODY
(from The Opera Ball).

VIOLIN.

HEUBERGER - KREISLER.

RÊVE D'ENFANT
DREAMS OF CHILDHOOD

VIOLON

by MAURICE DUPARLOIR

ITALIAN TWILIGHT
CRÉPUSCULE ITALIEN   DÄMMERUNG IM SÜDEN

VIOLIN SOLO

Arranged by the Composer
ALBERT W. KETÈLBEY

LULLABY

J. MORAVA

Recorded by MISCHA ELMAN on H.M.V.—DB 1396
O for the Wings of a Dove
(Les ailes de la Colombe)
TRANSCRIPTION

MENDELSSOHN—LUCAS

Russische Fantasie № 1
Russian Fantasia № 1   Fantaisie russe № 1

Violino

Leo Portnoff

Russische Fantasie № 2
Russian Fantasia № 2   Fantaisie russe № 2

Violino

Leo Portnoff

Zigeuner-Marsch.
Gipsies March.

VIOLINO.

O. Rieding, Op. 23. № 2.

Elfentanz.
Danse des Sylphes.

Violino.

E. Jenkinson.

Zingaresca.

VIOLIN.

GUSTAV ELLERTON, Op. 15. № 2.

The Grass-Hopper.
Dance.

VIOLIN.

BASIL ALTHAUS F.C.V.

STRING ORCHESTRA   STREICHORCHESTER
ORCHESTRE A CORDES   ORCHESTRA D'ARCHI

The following concertos and concertinos from the list are available with full string orchestral accompaniment:

Nachstehende Konzerte und Concertinos aus unserem Angebot sind mit voller Streichorchester-Begleitung lieferbar:

Les concertos et les concertinos de la liste suivante sont disponibles avec leur accompagnement d'orchestre à cordes:

I seguenti concerti e concertini come da lista sono disponibili con accompagnamento d'orchestra d'archi:

このリストにあるコンチェルトとコンチェルティノスは
すべて完全なストリング・オーケストラの伴奏付きです。

* Kuchler	Opus 12	* Portnoff	Opus 13	Seitz	Opus 15
* Kuchler	Opus 15	Rieding	Opus 34	Seitz	Opus 22
* Millies	(In the style of Mozart)	* Rieding	Opus 35	Ten Have	Opus 30

SELECTED PIECES FROM HANDEL edited by Felix Borowski

AUSGEWÄHLTE STÜCKE VON HÄNDEL herausgegeben von Felix Borowski

PIECES CHOISIES DE HAENDEL éditées par Félix Borowski

SELEZIONI DI PEZZI DI HÄNDEL curate da Felix Borowski

ヘンデル小品集 フェリックス・ボロウスキ 校閲

Bourree   Gavotte   Hornpipe   Largo   Menuet   Musette   Sarabande

*SIX VERY EASY PIECES in the First Position by Edward Elgar

*SECHS SEHR LEICHTE STÜCKE in der Ersten Lage von Edward Elgar

*SIX PIECES TRES FACILES dans la Première Position d'Edward Elgar

*SEI PEZZI MOLTO FACILI in Prima Posizione di Edward Elgar

＊やさしい小品6曲集 ファースト・ポジション エドワード・エルガー 校閲

All these are available with Piano, 1st Violin, 2nd Violin, 3rd Elementary Violin, 4th Violin (in lieu of Viola), Viola, 'Cello and Double Bass.
   * Also with additional parts for woodwind, brass and percussion.

Alle angeführten Werke lieferbar mit Klavier, 1. Violine, 2. Violine, 3. Violine (Obligat), 4. Violine (an Stelle von Viola), Viola, 'Cello und Kontrabaß.
   * auch mit zusätzlichen Stimmen für Holzblasinstrumente, Blechbläser und Schlagzeug.

Tous sont disponibles avec piano, 1er violon, 2ème violon, 3ème violon (élémentaire), 4ème violon (à la place de l'alto), alto, violoncelle et contrebasse.
   * Disponibles aussi avec les parties supplémentaires de bois, cuivres et percussions.

Tutti questi pezzi sono disponibili per pianoforte, primo violino, secondo violino, terzo violino semplice, quarto violino (al posto della viola), viola, violoncello e contrabasso.
   * anche con parti aggiuntive per strumenti a fiato, ottoni e strumenti a percussione.

これらはすべて、ピアノ、第1バイオリン、第2バイオリン、
第3エリメンタリー・バイオリン、第4バイオリン、ビオラ、
チェロ、ダブルベース のパート付きです。

　＊ウッドウインド、ブラス、パーカッションのパートもあります。

BOSWORTH